Bitcoin

Understand Cryptocurrencies, Bitcoin and Blockchain, How to Invest, Kkeep Your Coins Safe and Take Advantage from the Bitcoin Revolution

By

Simon Jordan

© **Copyright 2020 by Albrecht Meyer- All rights reserved.**

This document is geared towards providing exact and reliable information in regard to the topic and issue covered. The publication is sold with the idea that the publisher is not required to render accounting, officially permitted, or otherwise, qualified services. If advice is necessary, legal or professional, a practiced individual in the profession should be ordered.

From a Declaration of Principles which was accepted and approved equally by a Committee of the American Bar Association and a Committee of Publishers and Associations.

In no way is it legal to reproduce, duplicate, or transmit any part of this document in either electronic means or in printed format. Recording of this publication is strictly prohibited and any storage of this document is not allowed unless with written permission from the publisher. All rights reserved.

The information provided herein is stated to be truthful and consistent, in that any liability, in terms of inattention or otherwise, by any usage or abuse of any policies, processes, or directions contained within is the solitary and utter responsibility of the recipient reader. Under no circumstances will any legal responsibility or blame be held against the publisher for any reparation, damages, or monetary loss due to the information herein, either directly or indirectly.

Respective author(s) own all copyrights not held by the publisher.

The information herein is offered for informational purposes solely and is universal as so. The presentation of the information is without contract or any type of guarantee assurance.

The trademarks that are used are without any consent, and the publication of the trademark is without permission or backing by the trademark owner.

All trademarks and brands within this book are for clarifying purposes only and are the owned by the owners themselves, not affiliated with this document.

Table of Contents

INTRODUCTION 7

CHAPTER 1: UNDERSTANDING BITCOIN, BLOCKCHAIN AND CRYPTOCURRENCY 9

1.1 Defining Blockchain and Cryptocurrency 9

1.2 A Brief History of the Crypto Industry 11

1.3 The Three Pillars of Blockchain Technology 13

1.4 List of Famous Cryptocurrencies 15

1.5 Use of Bitcoin as a Currency 18

CHAPTER 2: MAINTAINING THE BLOCKCHAIN – NETWORK AND NODES 20

2.1 Why Do People Use the Peer-To-Peer Network? 21

2.2 The Use of Networks and Nodes in Cryptocurrencies 23

2.3 Who Uses the Blockchain? 28

CHAPTER 3: COMPARISON OF POPULAR CRYPTO EXCHANGES 31

3.1 What to Look for In an Exchange? 31

3.2 Comparison between Exchanges 35

3.3 Custodial Vs. Non-Custodial Exchanges 41

CHAPTER 4: EARN MONEY WITH BITCOIN AND OTHER CRYPTOCURRENCIES 45

4.1 Strategies to Consider while Buying Cryptocurrency 45

4.2 Bitcoin and Cryptocurrency Mining 46

4.3 Crypto Trading and its Strategies 51

4.4 Best Indicators for Cryptocurrency Trading 54

CHAPTER 5 TAKE BENEFITS OF THE MINING PROCESS 56

5.1 Digital Gold 56

5.2 Bitcoin Mining 57

5.3 Exploring the Mining Ecosystem 58

5.4 Proof of Work 60

5.5 Mining Rewards 62

5.6 Difficulty Metrics 62

5.7 Fees and Payout 65

5.8 Hardware Efficiency 66

5.9 Choosing a Currency 67

5.10 Trade/Exchange Rates 67

5.11 Requirements 68

5.12 The Payout Technique 71

5.13 The Pool Charges 71

5.14 Avoiding Large Pools 72

CHAPTER 6 INVESTIGATING ALTERNATIVE COINS .. 73

6.1 Open Source Cash: 74

6.2 The Ascent of the Altcoin 75

6.3 Conventions Based on the Bitcoin Blockchain 83

6.4 The Eventual Fate of Finance 84

CONCLUSION **86**

Introduction

A blockchain is an authentic record of every exchange confirmed by every computer in the system. Bitcoins and digital forms of money are made through a procedure called mining. Anybody can dig for most cryptographic arrangements of cash, yet it is a troublesome and tedious procedure. Mining includes groups of personal computers taking care of numerical issues. At the point when the item is tackled, tokens for which cryptographic money was being taken a shot at being made. For instance, a bitcoin, and the personal computers that got the arrangement gets the new token.

Mining is additionally what gives digital forms of money their security. The scientific issues that are being tackled are associated with the blockchain, the record of every token in cryptographic money. The most recent numerical issue does not only make more tokens; it additionally checks the most recent exchanges simultaneously. Bitcoins and different cryptographic currencies can be traded for products and enterprises similarly as British Pounds (£), American Dollars ($), the Euro (€) and different monetary standards you are utilized to.

To store and utilize your cryptographic money you will typically require a particular 'wallet' which will have its interesting computerized address, permitting you to send and get digital forms of payment. Notwithstanding wallets, you can likewise exchange your cash on trade. A portion of these will also permit you to change over your regular money - £, $, €, etc. - into digital money, and to turn over your property starting with one sort of cryptographic money then onto the next.

There are many authentic motivations to utilize digital money instead of regular monetary forms like British Pounds. It is protected, modest and quick and offers real specialized advancements that many accept will one day supplant more conventional types of trade. Because of the namelessness of the exchanges, they are added now and again utilized by crooks looking to stay away from discovery for unlawful exercises. Notwithstanding, individuals have been progressively purchasing cryptographic currencies for the reasons for the venture, planning to rake in some serious cash rapidly.

The flimsiness of digital forms of money does imply that it is conceivable to make enormous additions with limited quantities of ventures. As it turns out to be more incorporated into various degrees of our carries on with, it is nothing unexpected that expanded mindfulness is driving the developing budgetary unrest. While there are the two positives and negatives to electronic money, in all actuality there are sufficient large organizations and partnerships seeing approaches to coordinate the innovation and capitalize on its focal points, so the idea of advanced cash is not disappearing at an end soon. With variances in esteem making an ever-changing business sector for bitcoins and other, less well known, instances of cryptographic money, you might be taking a gander at the ideal ways that you can exploit the developing business sector and impact of this computerized force to be reckoned with.

Chapter 1: Understanding Bitcoin, Blockchain and Cryptocurrency

Blockchain holds a strong position in today's digital currency. Bitcoin is the name of the most popular digital currency, the one for which blockchain innovation was imagined. Cryptographic money is a vehicle of trade; for example, the US dollar, however, is computerized. It utilizes encryption procedures to control the production of commercial units and to confirm the exchange of assets.

1.1 Defining Blockchain and Cryptocurrency

Blockchain is an arrangement of recording data that makes it troublesome or difficult to change, hack, or cheat the framework. A blockchain is a record of electronic exchanges that are copied and circulated over the whole system of personal computer frameworks on the blockchain. Each block in the chain contains various trades, and each time another exchange happens on the blockchain, a record of that exchange is added to each member's career. The decentralized database overseen by various members is known as Distributed Ledger Technology (DLT).

Blockchain is a kind of DLT in which exchanges are recorded with an unchanging cryptographic mark called a hash. On the off chance that programmers needed to degenerate a blockchain framework, they would need to change each block in the chain, over the entirety of the appropriated adaptations of the chain.

The technology of Blockchain is a better approach for recording information on the web. This change can be used to form blockchain applications, for example, informal organizations, couriers, games, trades, stockpiling stages, casting ballot frameworks, expectation markets, online shops and substantially more. In this sense, it is like the web, which is the reason some have named it "The Internet 3.0".

Data stored on a blockchain can be converted to any form, regardless of whether it means an exchange of cash, possession, a transfer, somebody's character, an understanding between two gatherings, or even how much power light has utilized. In any case, it requires an affirmation from a few gadgets, for example, PCs, on the system. When an understanding, also called an accord, is reached between these gadgets to store something on a blockchain it is there, it cannot be contested, evacuated or modified, without the information and consent of the individuals who made that record, just as the more extensive network.

Digital currency is virtual money that is secured by cryptography, which makes it hard to be used for incorrect ways. Numerous cryptographic forms of payment are decentralized, which are dependent on blockchain technology, a dispersed record implemented by a different method of personal computers.

Digital currencies are structures that consider the protected instalments on the web, which are designated as virtual "signs," which are given by record passages interior to the framework. "Crypto" alludes to the different encryption calculations and cryptographic strategies that defend these passages.

Cryptographic money is advanced or virtual cash intended to function as a mode of trade. It utilizes cryptography to make sure about and confirm exchanges just as to control the formation of new units of specific digital money. Cryptographic forms of payment are restricted passages in a database that nobody can change except if conditions are satisfied.

There are a ton of vendors that acknowledge Bitcoin as the type of instalment. They extend from monstrous online retailers like Overstock and Newegg to little neighborhood shops, bars, and cafes. Bitcoins can be used to pay for lodgings, flights, jewelry, applications, PC parts and even advanced education.

Clients of cryptographic currencies other than Bitcoin can generally trade their coins for bitcoins. Additionally, there are Gift Card auctioning sites like Gift Off, which acknowledges around 20 distinctive cryptographic forms of money. Through gift vouchers, you can purchase anything with digital money.

1.2 A Brief History of the Crypto Industry

To comprehend the historical backdrop of digital currency development, we must make a speedy outing in "ancient times", to 1983. In those days, PC researcher and cryptographer David Chaum built up the primary mysterious electronic money application – Electronic Cash.

Electronic Cash permitted individuals to store their cash in a computerized position, and have it cryptographically marked by a bank. They could then utilize the money at any shop that acknowledged it, without opening a record with the seller.

In 1989, Chaum fused this framework into his electronic cash enterprise DigiCash Inc. DigiCash permitted automatic instalments to become untraceable and established the framework for mysterious exchanges. However, that was just the start. Right around ten years after the fact, everything was going to change with the distribution of a solitary whitepaper. In October 2008, an engineer (or gathering of designers) passing by the name of Satoshi Nakamoto, distributed a paper named "Bitcoin: A Peer-to-Peer Electronic Cash System". That is how the historical backdrop of digital money begins. After three months, on the third of January

2009, they discharged the first Bitcoin programming, and Nakamoto mined its beginning square (the first Bitcoin obstruct) for an award of 50 BTC.

Not like eCash, Bit Gold, and b-cash, but the Bitcoin was decentralized. This implies every one of its exchanges was recorded and dispersed over an extensive system composed of a great many PCs. The decentralization of Bitcoin implied that there was no focal overseeing authority, for example, a bank or an administration. After one year, in mid-2010, Nakamoto gave over the power over the bitcoin's source code vault and the system's alarm keys to Gavin Anderssen, one of the lead engineers in the bitcoin venture. He likewise moved different undertaking areas to significant individuals from the bitcoin network and ventured down from the bitcoin venture. The crypto business kept on snowballing all through 2015 and 2016. However, it was in 2017 when it truly sparkled.

Bitcoin's cost soared, coming to nearly $20,000 in December. Ethereum likewise detonated in esteem, beginning the year at $8.20 and finishing it at $755.27, with a development of over 9,000%. The market top of all digital forms of money available for use passed $100 billion by June 2017 and topped at $850 billion in January 2018. The vast market development of the crypto coins helped the business quickly gain notoriety. The web went haywire, and everybody got some answers concerning Bitcoin and cryptographic forms of money. An ever-increasing number of individuals began examining blockchain innovation and endless blockchain-based undertakings.

Although numerous social stages set up guidelines or out and out prohibited crypto ventures, the business discovered help in Telegram. Thus, ICOs likewise picked up notoriety and became feasible as well as an advantageous strategy for raising capital for tech organizations. The historical backdrop of digital currency does not end so quickly. After such development, the digital currency showcase swan made a plunge in January 2018. Bitcoin fell under $7000 hauling all altcoins with it. Before the end of November, digital money advertisements entered a great bear showcase. In the late spring of 2019, costs began rising once more, and 2020 started with a positively trending market too.

1.3 The Three Pillars of Blockchain Technology

The fundamental pillars of blockchain that has made it useable across the board approval are as per the following:

1- Decentralization

Before BitTorrent and Bitcoin went along, people were more used to bringing together administrations. The thought is fundamental. You have a strong element that puts away all the information and you would need to cooperate to get the data that is required. Another cause of a unified workflow is a bank. They keep all your money, and the best way that you can pay somebody is by experiencing the bank. Presently, unified frameworks have treated people well for a long time, notwithstanding, they have a few weaknesses. Now, as all the conventional workflows have a monopoly, all the information is put away in one spot. This makes them visible objective spots for expected hackers. In a decentralized workflow, the data is not put away by one single substance. Everyone in the system possesses the same data.

Decentralization implies such development that no directing authority can imply by any affiliations. This is ostensibly the chief component of crypto-development and blockchain innovation. You see what makes digital forms of money like Bitcoin notable. There is no regulating authority over it and can be used for trades wherever among the clients. Since decentralization does exclude such a focal center point and surrenders an arrangement of autonomous, customers, the possibility of Blockchain is simply the assortment of customers.

2: Transparency

The best concern for every person who includes digital money is its security. Here security implies both insurance and protection. No one will hazard such unsure stages for contributing. Albeit, different ways ensure that the people have secure access to their donated resources and one such strategy is the usage of crypto wallets, which have their one of a kind advanced area and can be a piece of online help arranges that partner you to a specific blockchain and empower you to buy and sell.

3: Immutability

Versatility describes the block chain's ability to manufacture its capacity at the same time keeping up smooth assignments. It intends to crash moderately dealing with times, swelling of frameworks, slacks, etc. Block chains, especially the Bitcoin blockchain, generally, gets more considerable and more significant considering its massive, unmistakable quality and request. This framework must be prepared to manage various trades each second. We are talking about an enormous number of businesses each second. Like this, to achieve this much stack of persistent worth-based data, better assets and systems must be executed. Blockchain is a connected rundown that contains information and a hash indicator that focuses on its past block, thus making the chain. This one little change is the thing that assembles block chains so incredibly reliable and exploring.

Suppose a hacker assaults block three and attempt to convert the information. Due to the features of hash works, a small change in data will convert the hash radically. This implies that any minor changes made in block three, will save the mixture which is put away in block two; presently that this will convert the information and the hash of block two which will bring about changes in block one etc. This breaks the chain, which is unthinkable. This is how block chains accomplish permanence.

1.4 List of Famous Cryptocurrencies

Digital currencies have not just changed the world's desires encompassing cash. They have additionally kept on advancing in their own way since the first Bitcoin block was mined in 2009. An ongoing study showed that 8% of Americans have placed funds into digital currency, and of that 8%, 5.15% have placed funds into Bitcoin.

Bitcoin (BTC)

For about ten years, Bitcoin extended money into the digital space of the internet. Since then, it has remained the most famous cryptographic money on the planet. With Bitcoin, users move cash beginning with one modern wallet then onto the next computerized storage of wallet effortlessly. Every trade is then checked by several users and kept on the open record, known as the blockchain. Even though it varies, its price is high. A single Bitcoin costs $4,931 U.S. dollars as of this structure. This is substantially higher than other cryptographic currencies that exist. Famous organizations are starting to acknowledge Bitcoins. This includes Microsoft, Overstock.com, and that is only the tip of the iceberg.

Bitcoin is supported by the most famous trades and modern wallet stages, for example, Coinbase. Financial experts have been favoring Bitcoin's advancement for quite a long time. Additionally, Bitcoin has the most noteworthy market monopoly among digital currencies, which is regularly noticed by experts. Market winners are determined by expanding the current flexibility of the cash by the current price. This is known as the flowing flexibility of money. Giant market tops, for the most portions, as there are more users. Therefore, Bitcoin is known to be a favorable decision than other cryptographic currencies.

Ethereum (ETH)

Setting the Bitcoin publicity aside, Ethereum is another well-known digital money. This digital currency utilizes a blockchain that is like Bitcoin's, however, has other money. Ethereum's cash is Ether, which gets oversaw by an open system of clients, almost the same as Bitcoin. The highest spot Ethereum fans out from Bitcoin are with its savvy contracts. These agreements are advanced agreements that pay clients directly after specific conditions get met.

Advantages of intelligent contracts for the most part are: You are dispensing with outsiders in exchanges. For instance, say you have a smart deal for your home. In a customary exchange, you would need a real estate professional to assist you with administrative work and intervene in transactions with the purchaser. Brilliant agreements, instead, move responsibility for a home to the purchaser without any other person's contribution. You additionally do not host to pay third gatherings, as you would a real estate agent.

You do not need to trust that administrative work will be processed. Savvy contracts are quicker and simpler. Everything is done on the web. You keep away from a lot of administrative work through and through. Exchanges get checked by several different clients. Notwithstanding your trades getting checked, they are additionally scrambled and put away on an open record. This helps keep a recorded history of your exchange, at last, making sure about it.

Ripple (XRP)

Most digital currencies are highly esteemed, giving quick exchanges. For Ripple and its electronic tokens are known as XRP, fast transactions are a center bit of their character.

Indeed, Ripple forms transfer in as meagre as four seconds. You can contrast this with Ethereum, which takes two minutes, and Bitcoin, which takes about 60 minutes. Common monetary standards can take a couple of days. Ripple works by making a stage for banks and other instalment suppliers to send cash the world over. XRP can be traded in any money. For example, it tends to be utilized for trades in dollars or euros. Having the option to send cash the world over in seconds permits banks and budgetary foundations to arrive at new markets. The farther their span goes, the more clients they can serve.

Litecoin (LTC)

Litecoin and Bitcoin share more practically speaking than merely the "coin" in their names: Litecoin has a blockchain, open record, and diggers who check exchanges. In any case, three key highlights make Litecoin stick out. This includes:

Litecoin forms transactions quicker than Bitcoin. Litecoin builds exchanges in about 2.5 minutes. Bitcoin preparing can take as long as 10 minutes. Litecoin has 84 million Litecoin altogether, contrasted with 21 million Bitcoins.

It has less mind-boggling calculations. Contrasted with Bitcoin, Litecoin has estimates that are simpler to break. This can make mining exchanges simpler to explain, and excavators additionally would not need as much gear to illuminate them as they would with Bitcoin.

Bitcoin Cash (BCH)

Although Bitcoin is the most famous digital money, which does not mean it comes without blemishes. Its family member, Bitcoin Cash, was made to help improve Bitcoin's adaptability, which influences exchange speed. This has prompted an increase in prominence for Bitcoin Cash. To help improve exchange speed, Bitcoin Cash expanded each square size from 1 megabyte (MB) to 8 MBs. Each square speaks to a rundown of exchanges that should be confirmed. Extending the square size permits more transfers to be checked at once. Expanding the number of exchanges that can be handled should help Bitcoin Cash contend with more substantial organizations, for example, PayPal and Visa. Moreover, Bitcoin Cash likewise intends to lessen exchange charges.

1.5 Use of Bitcoin as a Currency

Bitcoin is an only virtual currency or a vehicle of leading high-level exchanges, much the same as some other computerized cash. Recently, the worldwide enthusiasm for bitcoins has developed. Bitcoin and its choices are entirely founded on cryptographic calculations which are scrambled. This makes money decentralized offering proprietorship to the user. These can be bought through an online trade or a Bitcoin ATM. Milestone highlight of a bitcoin is that it can control the odds of misrepresentation and personality burglaries, and thus is viewed as an experimental method of holding money. Bitcoins permit purchasing of products and ventures on the web, just as moving cash.

Below are some of the advantages of utilizing bitcoins which makes it better than regular currency:

Bitcoin is a modern and decentralized cryptocurrency. Bitcoin gives access to the market without including middle people which means more noteworthy power of assets and fewer charges. It is faster, less expensive, safer, and changeless. Banks constrain money; on the other hand, bitcoin has possessors.

The simplicity of online trading: As we know, Bitcoin can help us in doing web-based shopping. It is like an electronic wallet which can convert blockchain technology to store, accompany and go through computerized cash.

Less unpredictable than currency: Bitcoin has a global acknowledgement and is slightly unstable than money. Because of this component, it gets more straightforward towards exchanges across limitations and on the web.

No exact method of monitoring regular cash the hidden innovation behind bitcoin. A great many PCs in a circulation utilize cryptographic procedures to make a lasting, open record of every Bitcoin exchange that has ever happened. This record will be entirely significant for different things other than the following instalment. In comparison, there is no suitable method for the next money.

Bitcoin is shared and open, yet secure and almost frictionless. Bitcoin permits trading an incentive over the web with no delegate and gives its clients access to their parity through a secret word known as a private key. So, it is closed, secure and at the equivalent time it is open.

Duplication incomprehensible - There is zero chance of duplicating a bitcoin, in contrast to money.

An excellent method of keeping up records for charge purposes: Once moved, a bitcoins' proprietorship likewise gets transferred. This implies two individuals cannot be executed on a similar worth, and this will help keep records stable and more straightforward, particularly for charge purposes.

Chapter 2: Maintaining the Blockchain – Network and Nodes

Bitcoin nodes speak with each other through the Bitcoin Peer to Peer arrange convention, and this way, they ensure the uprightness of the framework. A node that acts up or attempts to spread off base data is immediately perceived by the legitimate hubs and is disengaged from the system.

Regardless of the way that running an entirely approving hub does not give monetary prizes, it is energetically suggested because it provides trust, security, and protection to the clients. Full nodes guarantee that the principles are being followed. They secure the blockchain against assaults and fakes (for example, twofold spending). Likewise, a full node does not have to confide in others, and it permits the client to be in absolute control of his cash. Different forms of cryptographic, including Bitcoin, have been getting steam; the center has gone to blockchain the fundamental circulated record innovation (DLT) that controls these computerized monetary standards. Blockchain is advancing into apparently every industry.

Blockchain innovation is easy to comprehend at its underlying foundations. Fundamentally, the tech exists as a shared database loaded up with sections that must be affirmed by distributed systems and encoded. It is useful to imagine it as a firmly scrambled and shared Google Document, in which every passage in the sheet relies upon a legal relationship to every one of its forerunners and is settled upon by everybody in the system.

2.1 Why Do People Use the Peer-To-Peer Network?

In its least complicated structure, a distributed (P2P) organization is made when at least two PCs are associated and share assets without experiencing a different worker PC. A P2P system can be a specially appointed association—several PCs associated using a Universal Serial Bus to move documents. A P2P arrangement likewise can be a lasting framework that connects about six PCs in a little office over copper wires. Or then again, a P2P system can be a system on a lot more fantastic scope where uncommon conventions and applications set up direct connections among clients over the Internet.

The underlying utilization of P2P systems in business followed the sending in the mid-1980s of unsupported PCs. As opposed to the minima in frames of the day, for example, the VS framework from Wang Laboratories Inc., which presented word preparing and different applications to imbecilic terminals from a focal PC, put away records on a focal hard drive, and then-new PCs had independent hard drives and implicit CPUs. The savvy boxes additionally had installed applications, which implied they could be conveyed to work areas and be valuable without an umbilical string connecting them to a centralized server.

Numerous workers felt freed by having devoted PCs in their work areas. Be that as it may, soon they required an approach to share documents and printers. The conspicuous arrangement was to spare records to a floppy plate and convey the circle to the planned beneficiary or send it by official mail.

A Blockchain is a decentralized framework that utilizes distributed systems to implement value-based respectability just as security, and disposes of an outsider, for example, banks for intervention.

It offers a wide assortment of employments, and the quantity of utilizations which use it to mechanize honesty of exchanges for both commercial and non-monetary purposes has expanded over the previous decade. As such it has pulled in tremendous universal intrigue. A few nations are thinking about acquainting the Blockchain innovation with open administrations. Estonia has given e-Residency, a computerized ID that offers individuals everywhere throughout the world to begin an area free business. Their residents can likewise utilize it for casting a ballot in decisions, charge instalment, bank move, etc. The capability of Blockchain for nonmonetary exchanges and to stir up each significant division is undoubtedly enormous.

We additionally propose a novel coordination framework, Mariana, which is a decentralized worldwide deal framework. Trade is the beginning stage of all financial aspects. In a deal framework, exchange of merchandise happens legitimately for different products as opposed to a vehicle of trade, for example, cash. Until the only remaining century, it had been generally and broadly accepted from antiquated occasions that money was designed to tackle the burden of trade. Notwithstanding, numerous financial analysts and social anthropologists today are wary of this history among cash and deal. What we focus on in this part is not to include another perspective toward this discussion, however, to answer to build a genuine and worldwide monetary framework which is founded on a deal. This can encourage the presentation of a global non monetized economy that can flourish next to each other of the current adapted economy.

Our framework will be a distributed global deal framework, which will cause a piece of the universal economy to get a fresh start, and perhaps the leading authoritatively recorded economy which contains a worldwide deal exchange.

The center innovation supporting Mariana depends on a Blockchain, a consecutive appropriated database where exchange records are put away without experiencing a specific outsider. One might say, cash is an approved outsider intermediating between products or administrations, and a Blockchain expels such an outsider from the current framework. This framework will permit direct exchanges of items without experiencing a representative and without utilizing cash. In this framework, the significance of money will not be lost, and the execution of such a structure will permit our public to have it the two different ways: adapted economy and non-monetized economy.

2.2 The Use of Networks and Nodes in Cryptocurrencies

You can think about a hub (or fairly set of centers) as the establishment of a blockchain. If an electronic gadget has a working web association and as a matter, of course, an Internet Protocol (IP) address – it tends to be utilized as a hub. The essential capacity of a center is to hold a duplicate of the blockchain. Here and there a center can likewise be used to process an exchange. Significantly, every hub contains a copy of the blockchain since this characterizes the blockchain as both circulated and decentralized.

Hubs help guarantee that the respectability of the data is not changed. If somebody tries to alter the blockchain retroactively, it will just seem changed on that hub. The rest of the centers will show the 'valid' duplicate of the blockchain. This arranges the system as decentralized since no focal authority can have full power over the data being put away on a blockchain.

Bitcoin Nodes

Plunging into the setting of blockchains - which are structured as conveyed frameworks - the system of PC hubs is the thing that makes it workable for Bitcoin to be utilized as a decentralized distributed (P2P) advanced money. It is controlled safe by plan and does not require a center man to be executed from client to client (regardless of how far off they are on the planet).

Along these lines, blockchain hubs are liable for going about as a correspondence point that may perform various capacities. Any PC or gadget that associates with the Bitcoin interface might be considered as a hub as in they discuss some way or another with one another. These hubs are likewise ready to send data about exchanges and squares inside the conveyed system of PCs by utilizing the Bitcoin shared convention. Be that as it may, every PC hub is characterized by its specific capacities, so there are various sorts of Bitcoin hubs.

Full Nodes

Full nodes are the ones that genuinely bolster and give security to Bitcoin, and they are imperative to the system. These hubs may likewise be alluded to as entirely approving hubs as they take part during the time spent checking exchanges and squares against the framework's agreement rules. Additionally, full nodes can hand-off new transactions and squares to the blockchain. Generally, a full node downloads a duplicate of the Bitcoin blockchain with each square and exchange. However, this is not a prerequisite to be viewed as a full node (a diminished copy of the blockchain might be utilized).

A full Bitcoin node can be set up through various programming executions, yet the most utilized and famous one is the Bitcoin Core. These are the base necessities to run a Bitcoin Core full node:

- Work area or PC with an ongoing rendition of Windows, Mac OS X, or Linux.
- 200GB of free circle space.
- 2GB of memory (RAM).
- Fast web association with transfer paces of in any event 50 kB/s.

An unmetered association or an association with high transfer limits. Online full hubs may reach or surpass a transfer utilization of 200 GB/month and download use of 20 GB/month. You will likewise need to download ~200GB when you are beginning your full hub. Many volunteer associations and clients are running full Bitcoin hubs as an approach to help the Bitcoin biological system. Starting in 2018, approximately 9,700 open nodes are running on the Bitcoin organization.

Note that this number incorporates the open hubs, which allude to the listening Bitcoin hubs that are obvious and available (otherwise known as listening hubs). Other than the open node, there are numerous other shrouded hubs which are not noticeable non-listening hubs. These nodes are generally working behind a firewall, through concealed conventions like Tor, or basically because they were designed to not tune in for associations.

Listening Nodes (super nodes)

A listening node or super hub is a full hub that is freely obvious. It imparts and gives data to whatever another node that chooses to set up an association with it. Consequently, a super node is fundamentally a redistribution point that may demonstrate both as an information source and as a correspondence connection.

A dependable super node runs typically day in and day out. It has a few built-up associations, communicating the blockchain history and exchanges information to various nodes around the globe. Thus, a super node will likely require more computational force and a superior web association when contrasted with a full node that is covered up.

Miner Nodes

To have the option to mine Bitcoins in the difficult current situation, one needs to put resources into specific mining equipment and projects. These mining programs (programming) are not straightforwardly identified with the Bitcoin Core and are executed in corresponding attempts to mine Bitcoin squares. A digger may decide to work alone (solo excavator) or in gatherings (pool excavator).

While the independent excavators' full hubs utilize their duplicate of the blockchain, pool diggers cooperate, everyone, adding to his computational assets (hash power).

In a mining pool, just the overseer of the pool is required to run a full node- which can be alluded to as a pool excavator's full node.

Lightweight or SPV Customers

Otherwise called Simplified Payment Verification (SPV) customers, the lightweight customers are the ones that utilize the Bitcoin organization; however, do not generally go about as a full node. In this manner, SPV customers do not add to the system's security since they do not keep a duplicate of the blockchain and do not take an interest during the time spent checking and approving exchanges. To put it plainly, SPV is the strategy through which a client can check whether a few exchanges were incorporated or not in a block, without downloading the whole square information. In this way, SPV customers depend on the data given by other full nodes (super nodes). The lightweight customers fill in as correspondence endpoints and are utilized by numerous digital currency wallets.

Customer versus Mining Nodes

Note that running a full node is not equivalent to running a full mining node. While excavators need to put resources into costly mining equipment and programming, anybody can run an entirely approving node. Before attempting to mine a block, a miner needs to assemble pending exchanges that were recently acknowledged as legitimate by the full hubs. Next, the digger makes an up-and-comer obstruct (with a gathering of transactions) and attempts to mine that square. On the off chance that a digger figures out how to locate a substantial answer for their competitor square, they communicate it to the system with the goal that other full hubs can check the legitimacy of the square. Along these lines, the agreement rules are resolved and made sure about by the conveyed system of approving nodes and not by the miners.

2.3 Who Uses the Blockchain?

Be that as it may, blockchain innovation has a lot of more potential use cases past other than merely filling in as the fuel behind Bitcoin. Underneath, we have delineated a portion of its developing applications across money, business, government, and different enterprises.

Blockchain Use Cases in Banking and Finance

International Payments

Blockchain gives an approach to make a sealed log of delicate action safely and productively. This makes it incredible for global instalments and cash moves. For instance, in April 2018, Banco Santander propelled the world's first blockchain-based cash move administration. Known as "Santander One Pay FX," the administration utilizes Ripple's current to empower clients to make same-day or following day universal cash moves.

Via robotizing the whole procedure on the blockchain, Santander has decreased the number of mediators commonly required in these exchanges, making the process more effective. Like a vast business bank, Santander has various retail customers who might profit by more effective and less expensive instalments, especially in the region of global exchanges. Blockchain innovation can be utilized to diminish the expense of these exchanges by decreasing the requirement for banks to settle transfers physically.

Money Laundering Protection

By and by, the encryption that is so essential to blockchain makes it incredibly supportive in fighting illegal tax avoidance.

The hidden innovation engages record keeping, which underpins "Know Your Customer (KYC)," the procedure through which a business recognizes and confirms the characters of its customers.

Insurance

Seemingly the best blockchain application for protection is through keen agreements. These agreements permit clients and safety net providers to oversee claims straightforwardly and securely. All transactions and cases can be recorded on the blockchain and approved by the system, which would dispense with invalid arguments since the blockchain would dismiss numerous instances on a similar mishap.

Peer-to-Peer Transactions

P2P instalment administrations, for example, Venmo are advantageous. However, they have limits. A few administrations limit exchanges dependent on geology. Others charge an expense for their utilization. Many are defenseless against programmers, which is not engaging for clients who are putting their own money related data out there. Blockchain innovation, with all its previously mentioned benefits, could fix these detours.

Blockchain Applications in Business

Supply Chain Management

Blockchain's unchanging record makes it appropriate to errand, for example, continuous following of products as they move and change hands all through the flexible chain. Utilizing a blockchain opens a few choices for organizations moving these merchandises. Sections on a blockchain can be used for line up occasions with a graceful chain assigning merchandise recently showed up at a port to various steel trailers, for instance. Blockchain gives other and dynamic methods for sorting out the following information and putting it to utilize.

Healthcare

Wellbeing information that is reasonable for blockchain incorporates general data like age, sex, and possibly essential clinical history information like inoculation history or vital signs. All alone, none of this data would have the option to explicitly recognize a specific patient, which is the thing that permits it to be put away on a standard blockchain that could be gotten to by various people without unjustifiable security concerns.

Blockchain Applications in Government

Taxes

Blockchain tech could make the bulky procedure of documenting charges, which is inclined to human blunder, considerably more effective with enough data put away on the blockchain.

Non-Profit Agencies

Blockchain could take care of the counter trust issues noble cause are progressively looking through more prominent straightforwardness; the innovation can show benefactors that NPOs are in truth utilizing their cash as expected. Moreover, blockchain tech could help those NPOs recognize those assets more productively, deal with their assets better, and upgrade their following abilities.

Chapter 3: Comparison of Popular Crypto Exchanges

Exchanging Bitcoin or different digital currencies can be scary from the outset. There is usually news about tricks and individuals losing cash. While this is valid, and numerous methods have occurred and keep on happening, it has never been so easy to put resources into digital money. So much has progressed over the most recent couple of years that have made crypto exchanging sheltered and simple.

The premier concern, when exchanging and buying Bitcoin, or different digital forms of money, is wellbeing and security. Regardless of whether you mean to buy and hold long haul, need to exchange habitually, are keen on obscurity or safety, or essentially need convenience, the accompanying trades are the best for any utilization case you may have.

This rundown covers the best trades for specific sorts of brokers just as the best deals inside each kind of deal. There are various approaches to putting resources into Bitcoin or different cryptographic forms of money.

3.1 What to Look for In an Exchange?

Choosing the right cryptocurrency exchange might be one of the most significant beginning assignments an intrigued merchant or speculator must finish. Selecting an inappropriate stage might lead down a street filled with hacks, interruptions, and squandered exertion.

Investors may hope to spot trades. These are stages on which one can purchase and sell useful advanced resources themselves. Spot Bitcoin (BTC), for instance, is genuine Bitcoin that an individual can buy, sell, or move to any trade or wallet freely and hold for whatever length of time that is attractive.

Brokers, then again, may discover enthusiasm for subsidiaries — exchanging items, for example, prospects and alternatives that depend on the value activity of vital spot resources.

These items exchange contracts dependent on the value activity of hidden resources, and can be sunk into money or advanced resources, contingent upon the trade. These agreements are neighborhood to the deals facilitating them, which means they cannot be moved to different areas.

After the merchant has decided their targets, it becomes vital to investigate angles, for example, national guidelines, trade security and a large group of different perspectives. The following is a rundown of 10 significant regions to investigate while picking a trade.

1. Know Your Customer (KYC)

A few stages require KYC and AML to pull back assets or lift certain restrictions, committing clients to give duplicates of photograph recognizable proof and occasionally, a proof or living arrangement. Different stages require such client checks during the procedure of record creation. Numerous crypto trades these days likewise, boycott clients living in specific nations.

2. Reputation

Since the digital currency space is still generally another industry, it is critical to know about the notoriety of each trade of intrigue. Numerous businesses have been associated with loathsome exercises, hacks and leave tricks, leaving clients in not a precisely perfect circumstance. It is essential to direct research on various trades, looking through them on Google close by the expression "trick" and assessing the outcomes. Looking through the deal on different types of online life can likewise be valuable, hoping to check whether any objections have been posted.

Investigating every stage's terms and conditions can likewise be useful, taking note of whatever is disturbing or strange.

3. Security

Each trade has its own picked strategies for security. Verify whether the deal offers two-factor confirmation (2FA). The trade may not be worthy by security of the present guidelines. Google Authenticator, Authy and Yubikey are three normal roads for 2FA as they offer preferable security over versatile content based 2FA. Each trade likewise has different other safety efforts potentially worth looking into, for example, cool stockpiling resource holds and custodial stockpiling administrations.

4. Insurance fund

Users can note whether their business has protection support. Specific businesses have assets set up to reward clients under appropriate circumstances. Several businesses are secured under the Federal Deposit Insurance Corporation (FDIC), which can ensure a predetermined measure of U.S. clients' assets.

5. Fiat Exchange

Dealers and financial specialists sooner or later in their vocations likely will require a fiat good trade, permitting them to move national monetary forms (USD, CAD, and so forth.) into the crypto world for business use, and out of the crypto world for other benefits. A few trades have distinctive fiat choices, good with explicit banks, and some do not. Verifying which banks trades work with, just as what sorts of fiat monetary standards are tradable, might be vital.

6. Leverage trading

Subordinates trade much of the time and offer influence exchanging. Influence permits brokers to get a specific measure of assets for exchanges, considering the action of assets they hang on the trade. Influence might be significant for dealers hoping to enter momentary situations with a bigger size. Various trades offer somewhere in the range of 1x to 100x leverage, albeit different stages may have fluctuating standards regarding liquidation levels and edge calls.

7. Volume

Exchanging stages fluctuate depending on the number of members utilizing them at some random time, just as the measure of every benefit being transferred. This viewpoint can be significant as it influences how effectively clients can enter or leave positions. Suppose a dealer is hoping to sell 100 BTC. In that case, the person in question likely would not have the option to do as such on a low-volume trade as insufficient vendors may exist at the current recorded market cost, constraining the merchant to offer to bring down proposals on the business.

Volume issues regularly confound altcoin positions on specific trades, making it hard to purchase or sell a lot of those advantages. Checking volume can be a troublesome undertaking here and there, because of trades posting counterfeit capacity. One strategy includes taking a gander at the request book on various deals, observing what measures of every benefit sit in the request book and how far the value levels are from each other. Another approach to evaluate volume is to check outsider sites that offer this kind of information. Coin360, CoinMarketCap and OnChainFX are three alternatives that have various rundown volume information types.

8. Costs

Resource costs additionally fluctuate over numerous trades. Crypto resources may exchange higher or lower on one business versus another because of member area (China-based trades can occur occasionally siphon more), volume and different variables. Taking note of these errors can act as a factor in picking a deal, particularly when altcoins are concerned. Value error can likewise be a warning that a given trade may experience the ill effects of low volume.

9. Asset selection

Top advanced resources, for example, Bitcoin, Ethereum (ETH) and Litecoin (LTC) are broadly accessible on most crypto trades. Other littler top coins and tokens, be that as it may, may not be available on specific deals.

In this way, it tends to be essential to know which crypto resources each trade offers, making the suitable choices.

10. Fees

Most trades charge a little expense for each exchange. These charges change depending on the stage and are generally founded on a level of each transaction. Expenses may not be as critical to financial specialists as they are to brokers. Brokers purchase and sell more now and again, piling on charges more regularly, even though this relies upon the size of each exchange versus speculation measuring. A few trades additionally have withdrawal expenses and cutoff points.

3.2 Comparison between Exchanges

Here is a list of crypto exchanges based on the pros and cons which can be considered while buying cryptocurrency.

Bitcoin Exchange	30-day Volume ($)	Fiat Deposits	Mobile App	Margin Trading	Credit Cards
Poloniex	603M	No	Yes	Yes	No
Kraken	1.7B	Yes	No	Yes	No
Gemini	292M	Yes	Yes	No	No
Coinbase	2.1B	Yes	Yes	No	No
Bitstamp	1.2B	Yes	Yes	No	Not US
Binance	24.1B	No	Yes	No	Yes

1- Kraken

Established in 2011, it is the most significant digital money exchange and is an accomplice in the initial cryptographic currency bank. Kraken permits you to sell and purchase bitcoins, and trade between bitcoins and British Pounds, Canadian Dollars, US Dollars, euros, and Japanese currency. It is additionally conceivable to trade advanced monetary forms apart from Bitcoin for example Classic, ICONOMI, Montero, Ethereum, Augur REP index, Ethereum, Litecoin, Ripple, Dogecoin, Zcash, and Stellar. For professional clients, it offers edge exchange and a large category of other exchanging highlights. It is an incredible decision for more professional dealers.

On the other hand, crypto trade is established in San Francisco, USA, despite having one of the biggest Euro-to-crypto retails on the planet. Kraken is accessible to inhabitants of Canada, US, Japan, and different European countries.

Kraken as of now does not acknowledge stores using Visas, charge PayPal, cards, or comparable administrations. Kraken turned into the leading trade in 2014 on the planet with regards to Euro exchange volume. They additionally spearheaded the central apparent cryptographic verification of stores review framework and was likewise recorded on the Bloomberg end around the same time. It possesses a strong, yet non-learner cordial crypto exchanging stage.

2- Xcoins

Xcoins.com is a European-based driving digital money trade stage. Since its dispatch in 2016, the simple to utilize stage has served more than 250,000 fulfilled clients all over the world. Xcoins offers a snappy and secure answer for buying cryptographic forms of money all day, every day live help. They oblige tenderfoots, just as experienced crypto-veterans, and bolster more than 167 nations. With excellent client support and one of the speediest exchange forms, it is anything but difficult to perceive any reason why Xcoins has been developing exponentially since its origin. Regardless of your degree of experience or where you are on the planet, Xcoins.com is a protected and dependable approach to get your hands-on digital forms of money.

3-Coinbase

They are upheld by confided in financial specialists and utilized by a considerable number of clients internationally. Coinbase stage makes it easy to safely buy, use, store, and transfer computerized cash. Clients can buy bitcoins, Ether and now Litecoin from Coinbase through an advanced wallet accessible on Android and iPhone or through exchanging with different clients on the organization's Global Digital Asset Exchange (GDAX) auxiliary.

Crypto too and get cash straightforwardly into their financial balance. GDAX right now works in the United States, Europe, UK, Canada, Australia, and Singapore. GDAX does not presently charge any exchange expenses for moving assets between your Coinbase record and GDAX account. For the present, the choice of tradable monetary standards will, in any case, rely upon the nation you live in.

4-Cex.io

It is extraordinary compared to other cryptographic money trade that gives numerous instalment choices to use bitcoin and different digital currencies. This allows clients to trade fiat cash along with cryptographic currency effectively and similarly, digital currencies for fiat cash. Those who query to exchange bitcoins capably, the Cex.io offers trouble free exchanging dashboards and edge trading. Apart from that, this crypto trade likewise suggests a business administration that gives fledgling dealers in an incredibly straightforward manner to purchase bitcoin at costs that are very much focusing the retail rate. This is secure and intuitive, and digital currency can be kept in stockpiling.

5-ShapeShift

ShapeShift is one of the best digital money traders that underpins an assortment of cryptographic currency including Ethereum, Bitcoin, Zcash, Montero, Dogecoin, Dash and numerous others. It does not permit clients to buy crypto's with charge cards, Visas, or some other instalment framework. This crypto stage has none of the fiat strategy and considers the trade among bitcoin and other bolstered digital currencies.

6-Poloniex

The crypto trade offered safe trading ways with more than hundred distinctive Bitcoin currency partners and propelled devices. Poloniex uses a producer taker expense plan for all tradings, so charges are different for the creator. For creators, expenses run between 0 to 0.15%, contingent based on the total trade. Charges for takers are between 0.10 to 0.25%. There are zero expenses for taking out the exchange charge needed by the system.

7-Bitstamp

It is extraordinary compared to other bitcoin trade created in Europe. It was established in 2011 and stands in initial bitcoin trades that has developed an unwavering client base. This exchange is notable and trusted all through the bitcoin network as a protected exchanging stage. It offers propelled security highlights, for example, two-advance verification, multisig innovation for its storage and completely safeguarded cold stockpiling. Bitstamp has every minute of everyday assistance, and a multilingual UI and beginning is moderately simple. In the wake of creating a free record and forming a store, clients can begin exchanging right away.

8-CoinMama

This is an old crypto trade stage where everyone can go to buy bitcoin, using their Mastercard or money using MoneyGram. It is especially for the people who are required to create direct moment acquisition of advanced currency utilizing their nearby cash. Even though CoinMama's management is reachable globally, users ought to know that some nations will be not able to utilize all the features of this exchange. It is available in German, English, Italian, French and Russian.

In contrast to different trades, Coinmama does not contain an in-assembled wallet. If you need to exchange the cryptographic money trade, at that point, you should have your wallet for every one of the present digital currencies. While it urges clients to make their wallet, which is significantly safer, it is not the most helpful alternative.

9-Bitsquare

It is easy to understand shared trade that permits you to purchase and trade bitcoins in return for fiat monetary forms or digital currencies. It retails itself as a genuinely decentralized and distributed trade that is immediately available and needs no requirement for enrollment or dependence on a focal power. It never contains client reserves and anybody except exchanging accomplices' trade individual information. The stage offers incredible privacy with multisig addresses, privacy stores and reason manufactured mediator framework if there should be an occurrence of exchange debates. On the off chance that you need to stay mysterious and do not confide in anybody, Bitsquare is the ideal stage for you.

10-Binance

If a trader's center is to direct crypto-to-crypto exchanging, Binance is perhaps the ideal choice. They are placed as well-known digital money trades around the world; they give you noteworthy contributions alongside an incredibly low exchanging charge. Even though the Binance stage is a youthful contestant into retail, it is quickly developing and holds an enormous choice of altcoins with Ethereum, Bitcoin and Tether bindings.

It offers a coin named BNB (Binance coin). Being an incorporated trade, you can achieve proper limits while leading exchange with their index.

It provides a standard exchanging expense of just 0.1% which can also be decreased more if the instalment is made within BNB.

12- Huobi

For now, Huobi is just accessible to Chinese and US inhabitants barring those living in Arizona, New York, Alabama, Georgia, Connecticut, Louisiana, North Carolina, Vermont, Hawaii, Washington, and other U.S. Regions. Huobi offers plenty of token exchanging choices.

It underpins a full scope of digital currencies and ICO index that includes every single significant coin like bitcoin (BTC), Bitcoin Gold (BTG), (DASH), (EOS), Bitcoin Cash (BCH), Ethereum Classic (ETC), Ethereum (ETH), Lisk (LSK), Litecoin (LTC), ICON (ICX), (NEO), (QTUM), Ripple (XRP), NEM (XEM), Tether (USDT), Tron (TRX), Zcash (ZEC), and so forth. It is giving more than hundred altcoins exchanging sets and offers to trade by BTC, USDT and ETH. Aside from Huobi.pro, the institute has additionally propelled Huobi Autonomous Digital Asset Exchange (HADAX). On the other hand, the expert site lists over hundred digital currencies and tokens, HADAX, however, is only over a couple of month's old records an extensive exhibit of little coins and indexes. HADAX permits dealers to decide in favor of the symbols they need to view on the stage by utilizing Huobi tokens.

3.3 Custodial Vs. Non-Custodial Exchanges

Custodial

Coinbase, GDAX, Kraken, Binance, Bitfinex, Poloniex are known for custodial trades. They are notable and have gigantic measures of crypto travelling through their foundation.

These exchanges possess your crypto; they are the overseers of your personal keys. Exchanging is done off-chain, implying that exchanging is followed on their asset report as opposed to being confirmed by the blockchain. This permits exchanges to be done rapidly and efficiently however prompts an absence of straightforwardness.

Record enlistment and character confirmation are likewise reserved for these sorts of trades. This eases back the exchanging procedure as well as empowers you to confide in the business with touchy data, for example, your Social Security Number. Exchanging your altcoins for different altcoins can likewise be irritating. For instance, possibly you have Montero, and you need to purchase Dash. You would need to sell your Montero for something like Bitcoin initially and afterwards utilize your Bitcoin to obtain Dash (investing more energy and paying more expenses).

There are a few preferences to utilize these sorts of trades, such as having the option to store and withdraw fiat cash, high exchange volume, and frequently more top cutoff points.

Even though these trades are broadly utilized, numerous individuals feel like things could be better. Indeed, even the most legitimate names like Coinbase experience timeframes where access to reserves is inaccessible (site accidents or support). Individuals, despite everything, make the slip-up of leaving their money on a trade as opposed to moving it into cold stockpiling or to a safe multi-coin wallet like Comfy.

There are numerous reasons why individuals are endeavoring to investigate options in contrast to this sort of trade, from charges of market control and insider exchanging to forks not being perceived.

They are seen by some just like the "huge banks" of the crypto space and causing a unified impact.

Numerous individuals feel like the cons exceed the masters, which is the reason some have been working enthusiastically to make another period of exchanging. Custodial trades are to be sure prevailing in the crypto space. Their exchange volume is unusual. However, their predominance has blurred some because of elective arrangements being presented.

Non-Custodial

The way that no record is required for exchanging makes this model ideal for individuals who need to finish a lively exchange. It is additionally useful for people who would prefer not to focus on a trade or who are reluctant to depend on the deal with individual data. The earth considers a further extent of namelessness and security. An exchange is made in a split second for your benefit, and a non-custodial trade does not hold your cash as a custodial one does. After a brief timeframe, the crypto is consequently kept in your ownership.

Even though Shapeshift is the most notable case of a non-custodial trade, a couple of imperative contenders exist. Changelly and Evercoin are additionally feasible choices. In any case, another option known as Switchain gives a stunningly better-exchanging experience. What sets Switchain separated is the way that it has its own exchange sets accessible. However, it looks at rates across trades to ensure you generally get the best arrangement. This makes non-custodial trades much more tempting as minimal effort exchanging joined with protection and accommodation offer a prevalent exchanging elective.

Decentralized Exchange

A third alternative to execute crypto is to utilize a decentralized trade. This sort of deal despite everything has a moderately little exchange volume yet it is developing, regardless of being in its formative stages.

The thought is to have an open-source, permission less on-fasten stage for exchanges to happen. Even though hindrances are easing back progress (scalability and charges, for instance), the interest for such a trade is yet substantial. Etherdelta and IDEX are two notable models.

Exchanging is finished using savvy contracts on the Ethereum arrange as opposed to being done on a brought together stage. Ethereum tokens are exchanged on these trades (Ethereum is not the main stage supporting decentralized businesses, yet it is the most common).

Albeit believing an outsider is not essential, a great deal of confidence is put on the brilliant agreement itself. Cash can and has been taken from decentralized trades notwithstanding the way that numerous network individuals thought of them as not hack able.

There is likewise an idea called cross-chain nuclear trading which would permit cryptographic forms of money on various block chains to be exchanged in a decentralized style. Useful atomic trades have happened. However, there are limitations, and an item that permits this transfer has not ultimately shown at this point.

Chapter 4: Earn Money with Bitcoin and Other Cryptocurrencies

There are many approaches to get money with cryptographic currency and generate money in the crypto area. Putting resources into Bitcoin can appear to be confusing; however, it is a lot simpler when you separate it into steps. You do not need to learn programming to understand that bank. Cryptographic mining is a process where trading for different types of digital currency are confirmed. This includes it to the blockchain computerized record. To be serious with varying miners of crypto, however, a digital currency excavator needs a PC with specific equipment.

4.1 Strategies to Consider while Buying Cryptocurrency

Assessing cryptocurrency requires some investment and exertion to do right. It is fresh out of the box new industry, and its fast development has made numerous changes yet, also various risks for financial specialists.

Staking and Lending

Staking and Lending allow financial specialists to present cash with altcoins. Trademark implies securing coins, cryptographic money storage and accepting reimbursements to allow trading on a Proof of Stake (PoS) organization. Other than mining, the PoS calculation gets trade supporters who are dependent on the number of coins they resolved to stake. Proof of Stake does not need expensive tools and is more productive. Similarly, cold marking is an alternative, allowing financial experts to stake coins while keeping them in safe disconnected storage. NEO, Stellar (XLM), and Tie are sections of the coins you can stake.

Financial experts are lending coins to the system, to confirm its security and sustain trading. Another alternative to gain cash with crypto is to lend coins to other financial experts and create passion on that advance. Several platforms support crypto lending, including exchanges, distributed lending platforms and decentralized currency (DeFi) features.

Mining

Mining is an essential portion of the Proof of Work (PoW) agreement component and is nearly the most seasoned method of getting money with crypto. It is a process of confirming trading and ensuring a Proof of Work arrangement. Miners are compensated with new coins, through block prizes, for playing out these areas. At the start of Bitcoin, mining was practicable on a workstation yet today needs specific mining tools. Regarding the business of assisting a system, running a master node can similarly be profitable. Both strategies need exclusive ability and critical forthright and progressing speculation.

4.2 Bitcoin and Cryptocurrency Mining

The extract for a few Bitcoin miners is the chance of being rewarded with necessary bitcoin tokens. You surely are not required to be an excavator to claim digital currency signs. You can similarly buy cryptocurrency utilizing fiat cash. You can even win it through system games or by spreading blog appearances on platforms that pay users in cryptographic currency.

The bitcoin gift that miners receive is a motivator which persuades people to play the primary part of mining: to assist, legitimize and play the Bitcoin system and its blockchain.

These duties are divided between several clients all around the globe. Bitcoin is a "decentralized" cryptographic currency that does not depend on a government or national bank to direct its guidelines.

- By mining, you can win digital currency without putting down cash for it.
- Bitcoin excavators get bitcoin as an award for finishing "hinders" of confirmed exchanges which are added to the blockchain.
- Mining rewards are paid to the excavator who finds an answer for a complex hashing puzzle first. The likelihood that a member will be the one to find the arrangement is identified with the part of the total mining power on the system.
- Twofold spending is a marvel wherein a bitcoin client illegally spends similar tokens twice.
- It would assist if you had either a GPU (illustrations handling unit) or an application-explicit coordinated circuit (ASIC) to start a mining rig.

Cloud Mining

Cloud mining is where you pay somebody (frequently it is a significant partnership) a measure of cash and "lease" their mining machine called a "rig", and the way toward mining itself. The individuals or organizations that offer these cloud mining administrations typically have colossal mining offices. These offices are with different homesteads (tens or several apparatuses stacked and working together) at them and realize entirely well how to mine cryptographic money. Cloud mining has been mainstreamed for the most part since it offers the likelihood to take part in the realm of digital currency.

There are two alternatives to cloud mining - free and paid. Usually, many individuals that are searching for approaches to mine cryptographic money would float towards the "free" options. However, it has its downsides (extremely moderate mining speeds, additional conditions, and so forth.). Paid cloud mining, for the most part, works this way:

You discover a cloud mining host on the web. You look at the plans that the host offers - there are generally four or five of these plans, going from the least expensive to the most costly one; a few have much to provide you with the capacity to make and redo your cloud mining plan. When you realize what you need, you mostly play out the exchange (implying that you pay the host), register your digital money wallet code, and that is how you make the initial steps on the most proficient method to mine cryptographic money.

Various plans cost various measures of cash and keep going for an assortment of periods. The standard methods can go somewhere in the range of $500 up to $5000, and last from two years to a lifetime.

It is typically expected that you will earn back the original investment after one year and afterwards start gaining profit. The costs of digital forms of money are volatile and their prices will generally be influenced by a considerable amount.

CPU Mining

CPU mining uses processors to mine digital forms of money. It used to be a feasible choice some time ago; however, at present, less and fewer individuals pick this technique for mining digital currency day. Most importantly, CPU mining is moderate. You could continue for quite a long time without seeing the littlest increase of income.

It is additionally ordinarily not justified, despite any potential benefits - you make next to no measures of cash; however, you most likely burn through multiple times that sum on power and cooling. The issue mitigates itself by a piece on the off chance that you can discover a spot that has pleasant cooling and modest power bills.

All you should have the option to mine utilizing the CPU technique is only a PC and a few projects. It is conceivable to do it with a PC, yet it is not advised. Your PC will likely sear and overheat in a matter of a few hours. The way that it is so natural to begin digital money mining pulls in new CPU excavators consistently. A few people that are searching for how to mine digital money could not care less about the subtleties - they need to begin the procedure at the earliest opportunity, and in any conceivable capacity.

GPU Mining

GPU mining is likely the most mainstream and notable strategy for mining cryptographic forms of money. If you google "digital currency mining", GPU rigs will be a portion of the first things that you will see. Cloud miners, for instance, use GPU rigs for their administrations. Furthermore, these folks are experts that occasionally have hundreds if not many apparatuses. GPU mining is well known because it is both practical and moderately modest. Try not to misunderstand me, the development of the apparatus itself will, in general, be expensive. However, with regards to its hash speed and the overall workforce, the GPU mining rig is incredible. GPU rigs use illustration cards to mine digital forms of money. One conventional apparatus is made from a processor, a motherboard, cooling, rig outline and - obviously - two to eight (2 - 8) design cards.

An average cost for a well-performing and pleasantly manufactured GPU mining rig expects to be around the $3000 value extends.

Its massive speculation however will take care a lot quicker than, suppose, a CPU digger. Individuals searching for ways to mine cryptographic money should look at it.

ASIC Mining

ASICs (Application-Specific Integrated Circuits) are unique gadgets that are planned unequivocally to play out a solitary undertaking, which for this situation is crypto mining. ASICs are very notable and cherished because they produce crazy measures of cryptographic money when contrasted with its rivals' GPU and CPU. For this particular reason, they are a significant subject of debate.

When the ASIC organization reported its new form of the machine, the declaration created a scene in the digital money network. Since ASICS are so incredible, they ransack different excavators who are utilizing GPU or CPU apparatuses of the likelihood to keep up both in hash speeds and in profit. Likewise, ASICS has contorted the economy of certain digital forms of money envisioning if most of the benefit would go to one excavator with an ASIC ranch, what sort of disorder that would follow.

Best Mining Technique

In case you are searching for crypto mining ways, cloud mining is likely the most well-known path to mine digital currencies without making the slightest effort. To start mining and enhance the hub inside the shared system and begin making Bitcoins requires a computer with web access. This requires some level of due perseverance like the occurrence with a venture. In mining pools, the organization administrating the mining pool demands an expense. While mining pools are equipped for settling a few obstructions every day, miners should be given a piece of a mining pool moment income.

4.3 Crypto Trading and its Strategies

With the correct exchanging technique, you stand a greatly improved difference in producing an arrival on your speculation. As you think about your procedure, there are a few key things to remember about the digital money market. A factor that drives the instability of the crypto to advertise is the way that the innovation behind it – blockchain – is new and evolving. As the estimation of the change to enterprises outside of the digital currency commercial center increments, so does the opinion of cash.

Only invest money you can have the power to lose.

Cash esteems go all over rapidly. Blockchains and cryptographic forms of money can be influenced by hacks and bugs that decline in an incentive in unexpected ways. The customary securities exchange has swings; however, if you hold your positions and use sound judgment, it is uncommon to see significant misfortunes after some time. Be that as it may, with digital money, the danger of losing cash is a lot higher. Avoid any risks.

Do your research: #DYOR.

Doing your own research is extremely significant for cryptographic money. Exploration of the monetary forms you are thinking about purchasing to ensure they meet your venture objectives, while likewise being organizations whose crucial help. Keep in mind, an interest in cryptographic money is an interest in the organization that produces it, just as an interest in blockchain innovation.

Avoid FOMO (Fear of Missing Out)

There is a great deal of promotion around digital currencies. This can prompt individuals purchasing coins at a significant expense, possibly to lose cash if the money's worth drops.

Try not to put resources into a payment because there is a massive buzz around it.

Diversify your portfolio

You can settle on choices about which coins to put resources into – there are more than 1,500 cryptographic forms of money available. Most of the time with stocks, it is suitable to have some sure things alongside any less secure speculations you need to make.

Take profits at intervals. If you watch the digital currency advertise intently, you will see that qualities can increment and diminish whenever. In case you are doing momentary exchanging and see an enormous increment in esteem, you should check whether the worth will increment significantly more. Be that as it may, nothing is exempt from the forces of gravity. So, by setting up a system where you are taking benefits at average spans, you improve your probability that you will see consistent returns.

Trading points

Long-term trading

When utilizing a drawn-out exchanging technique for contributing to the securities exchange, an individual can depend on the chronicled information to settle on a choice. That is not generally the situation for digital currency as there is just a constrained measure of data accessible. The methodology could demonstrate exceptionally gainful to putting resources into digital forms of money that have been around for a couple of years.

Short-term trading

Momentary exchanging adopts the contrary strategy to long haul exchanging. It intends to produce an arrival on an interest in a brief timeframe. In a perfect world, you contribute, the cost goes up and you sell for benefit.

Technical analysis

Specialized Analysis is a strategy for examining money by exploring factors identified with estimations of connected resources previously and current commercial center by authentic volume and value information. Necessarily, it is a methodology based on the possibility that the previous will foresee the future, so it utilizes past exhibitions as an advantage for anticipating how a stock will act later. You can do a specialized examination of liquid by using the scope of diagramming apparatuses accessible.

Fundamental analysis

Essential investigation plans to distinguish the estimation of money depends on the basics of the undertaking. The test with applying necessary research to digital forms of payment is that cryptographic arrangements of cash are not of companies. They do not have open budget summaries. Their reasonability relies upon the quality of the network in the system. You can start a primary examination by looking for our activity's whitepaper, which will layout objectives and usefulness. You can likewise search for content on the digital money's blog or other network discussions, like Reddit. Building up a technique for putting resources into cryptographic money does not ensure achievement. You must keep awake-to-date on the changing business sector and any pertinent news, actualize your method all the time, and be sure you make the best, most educated choices conceivable.

4.4 Best Indicators for Cryptocurrency Trading

Here, we will feature the absolute best, least demanding to learn, and the best of the specific investigation markers that work best for digital currencies like Bitcoin, Ethereum Ripple, Litecoin, and EOS. When you have aced how these devices work over the digital currency advertise, these apparatuses can likewise assist merchants with getting a severe edge in forex, wares, stocks, and that is only the tip of the iceberg. That is the reason it merits investing energy honing your exchanging abilities and learning everything to think about hazarding the board.

Relative Strength Index Crypto Trading Strategy

The Relative Strength Index is the critical marker we will disclose because it is so direct to use for a successful, benefit producing exchanging system that yields typically positive outcomes. Dealers can change this dependent on their solace levels, for a more severe or free methodology, contingent upon their hazard hunger. The most traditionalist passages forestall misfortunes. However, just the most outrageous moves will be exchanged. The RSI can finish off merchants when patterns are coming up short on the force. An inversion could follow and demonstrate when a benefit is right now oversold or overbought. The RSI is anything but difficult to peruse, and considerably simpler to use to fabricate an effective exchanging technique.

Moving Average Convergence Divergence (MACD) Strategy

The MACD is a most loved among crypto brokers, as it can frequently give an early sign of when an inversion might be coming as the lines turn, later affirming the flag when a hybrid happens.

The MACD is usually alluded to as a slacking marker and is among the most generally utilized specialized investigation pointers in presence. The instrument can enable dealers to foresee when pattern changes are going to occur. Short for the Moving Average Convergence Divergence pointer, it is a specific examination marker made by creator and broker Gerald Appel in the last part of the 1960s. The device gives very simple to understand flags and incorporates a histogram to additionally help merchants with providing a visual portrayal of the quality of a pattern; thus, the hybrids are unmistakably characterized. Nonetheless, because of the MACD being a slacking pointer, it can give false readings that can affect brokers by taking positions sooner than justified.

Bollinger Bands Strategy

Utilizing the straightforward midline moving average of the Bollinger Bands as a trigger for long or short signals, can end up being a consistent, effective system for crypto dealers. Bollinger Bands were made by eminent monetary expert John Bollinger in the mid-1980s however, remain incredibly well known even today. The specialized investigation pointer comprises two plotted standard deviation lines and a necessary moving regular. At the point when the groups fix, instability has dropped flagging that a flood in unpredictability is standard and a break of the range is likely. "Riding the groups," in any case, can be gainful, however just if the value breaks out of the band with a massive flood of volume.

Chapter 5 Take Benefits of the Mining Process

The Bitcoin organization disseminates recently stamped bitcoin through a novel methodology called Mining. By willfully providing crude registering power, excavators serve the system by approving and affirming Bitcoin exchanges. Consequently, the diggers are granted bitcoins from a constrained gracefully. Alongside each grant, they take charges according to the trades they decide to approve. Bitcoin mining, a significant part of the system, is severe and includes numerous specialized variables. In this section, we will investigate the mining procedure in more detail. With this base comprehension of the process, we will have the option to comprehend the practicality of mining.

5.1 Digital Gold

The first people surely had a favorable position concerning finding valuable materials, for example, gold and silver. It is anything but complicated to envision chips or little pieces of gold usually uncovered by streams and lakes. Individuals strolling around the zone could without much of a stretch gather them for exchange or utility. As time went on, increasingly more of the effectively accessible valuable metals and diamonds were picked. Diggers proceeded with their pursuit more profound into the earth, taking a chance with their lives and riches in a search for these essential materials. With the development of human progress to new terrains and mainland's, new sources were found. In 1849, gold was found in a stream close to Coloma, California. After the news broke, a vast number of excavators, called the 49ers, surged out to California looking for the gold.

Within some years, most of the handily discovered gold was picked, driving the diggers to utilize further developed methods. By the mid-1850s, the diggers had embraced pressure-driven mining hardware, and other mechanical intentions to remove the gold. It was a troublesome procedure, and active mining required ability and luck.

5.2 Bitcoin Mining

The 1849 California Gold Rush is practically equivalent to the start of Bitcoin's mining story. The two of them share comparative qualities. In the first place, both gold and bitcoin are restricted gracefully. The measure of gold on the planet is fixed and cannot increment. Likewise, Bitcoin's calculation is intended to guarantee that a fixed standard of bitcoin will be found. In the two cases, the early diggers would be wise to result in mining first and foremost. With Bitcoin mining, the quantity of bitcoins granted to the diggers diminishes after some time. The new prize block parts at regular intervals and the mining trouble increments, as it is balanced at regular intervals considering the opposition to mine. Therefore, numerous early adopters had the option to effectively mine more than 50 bitcoins a day utilizing a standard PC with a quick PC or a designs processor. Today, digging for gold is a costly activity and is commonly left to large mining organizations subsidized by huge ventures of capital. Same is the case with Bitcoin Massive mining organizations and pools exist, driving the opposition to discover bitcoin way up.

The brilliant long periods of Bitcoin mining might be behind us. However, the move toward mining despite everything assumes a significant job in the Bitcoin biological system. Notwithstanding winning recently printed bitcoins, the excavators likewise take exchange charges.

These charges are paid by the sender of a bitcoin exchange and make a motivation for the excavators to affirm their transaction rapidly.

Having an enormous base of diggers is critical to Bitcoin as it assembles trust in the system.

The bigger the support of diggers, the more troublesome it is to overwhelm the system. As we have seen with a considerable lot of the altcoins that have been delivered, with no significant base of excavators, there is almost no trust in the money. At last, it yields a low conversion standard with little interest in the capital.

5.3 Exploring the Mining Ecosystem

Bitcoin mining furnishes the system with two significant procedures: the formation of new bitcoin and the affirmation of transactions. Understanding the Blockchain, the excavators tune in for new and legitimate exchanges to join them into another block. The block speaks to a degree around a gathering of transactions that can be handily approved against the past blocks.

Organizing the record this way prepares for exchanges simple to distribute. From the excavator, another block is conceivably famous. The bytes from the block are utilized as the base for figuring a response to a troublesome processing issue.

The diggers make a vast number of endeavors at taking care of the annoying figuring issue in anticipation of finding the arrangement before some other miner.

If found, the excavator rapidly communicates the answer for the system to make the case.

If it is affirmed by the system, the excavator gets the new bitcoin, just as all the charges included with every exchange in the block.

The new block at that point fills in as the most recent block in the blockchain. The excavators at that point start the race again by tuning in for further exchanges and rehashing the procedure.

Every exchange communicated to the system must be checked for twofold spending, that is, sending more bitcoin than what is accessible, and for a legitimate advanced mark. To affirm the available equalization, the digger must have an approved duplicate of the whole blockchain. Installing a Bitcoin Node, after establishment, a customer will interface with the system and start mentioning each block consecutively from different hubs on the network. In the wake of checking each block against the past blocks, individually, the blockchain is reproduced and put away locally.

Must be checked for twofold spending, that is, sending more bitcoin than what is accessible, and for a substantially advanced mark. To affirm the available equalization, the digger must have an approved duplicate of the whole blockchain.

Installing a Bitcoin Node, after establishment, a customer will interface with the system and start mentioning each block successively from different hubs on the network.

After checking each block against the past blocks, individually, the blockchain is imitated and put away locally. The nearby duplicate of the blockchain contains each exchange from the earliest starting point of time. This record is kept up and used to approve the spending parity of each new exchange. If an exchange is seen as invalid, it is mostly disregarded and discarded.

The second check requires the approval of the advanced mark. Utilizing cryptographic calculations, the digger can check the score joined to the exchange to approve the uprightness of the transfer.

Any adjustment to the assignment will bring about an invalid mark, and subsequently, the digger can affirm that the exchange to be handled was the first form sent from the holder of the private key. With a rundown of substantial exchanges, the excavator collects another block and uses it as the base for unravelling a troublesome processing problem.

5.4 Proof of Work

Understanding the Blockchain, we depicted a hash as the consequence of a scientific capacity applied to a lot of information. For our situation, the information is the new block of legitimate exchanges. At the point when a hashing capacity is used to the report, a numerical worth is returned. If we change any byte of the information and recomputed the hash, we will get new hash esteem that is fundamentally unique to the first.

Mining includes utilizing the hash capacity to create a hash result. If the hash result coordinates the objective, it is viewed as the arrangement. The outcome is invalid, an expendable number called a nonce is added to the information. The informational index is then hashed once more, giving the excavator another attempt. This procedure is rehashed until an answer is found.

At the point when an answer is discovered, it is communicated to the system as another block, which additionally contains the trouble target and the triumphant nonce. This is called evidence of-work. Different hubs on the network can recomputed the hash on the block and the nonce to check the evidence of-work.

Whenever acknowledged, the new block turns out to be a piece of the blockchain. The hubs that concur on the arrangement at that point share the original block with different centers on the system.

The final products are the new bitcoins and the exchange charges gathered are granted to the winning miner.

Registering hash esteem is computationally costly. To deliver the evidence of-work, the hashing capacity is executed commonly until a legitimate hash is found. Subsequently, the work is depicted as "comprehending a troublesome figuring problem". Bitcoin utilizes a hash work called SHA-256. It is a safe cryptographic hash work that can be registered by programming or more effectively by hardware. Specifically, the diggers are searching for hash esteem that is not precisely the objective worth. They will perform many hashes every other searching for the triumphant hash result. Since any little change to the informational collection creates alternate hash esteem, a nonce is added to the set. Each retry of the hash incorporates an addition to the nonce. When increased, the subsequent mixture is extraordinary to the past hash. This gives the digger one more opportunity at finding hash esteem that is lower than the distributed trouble level.

Scrypt

Litecoin, just as numerous other altcoins, utilizes an alternate arrangement for the hashing calculation. Scrypt likewise uses SHA-256 for hashing, however with an extra estimate called Salsa20, which requires a lot of memory, or RAM, to figure. Consequently, the scrypt calculation is not just computationally costly; it is mind serious too.

The method of reasoning behind utilizing an extra part, for this situation, a lot of RAM, is to make it harder to scale the mining procedure using PC processors alone. This gives those with access to singular PCs a favorable position over the mining activities that scale with processors.

5.5 Mining Rewards

Newly stamped bitcoins are granted for confirmation of-work affirmed by the system. The quantity of bitcoins awarded is determined to a bend, which parts every 210,000 blocks. The first rewards were set at 50 bitcoins. After around four years, the initial 210,000 blocks were mined, and the prize was diminished considerably to 25. The rate will keep dividing, to 12.5, 6.25, etc., until the last division of a bitcoin is found.

The bend, which decreases fifty-fifty after some time, is planned to balance the foreseen increment in accessible registering power as the expense of figuring power diminishes the trouble of acquiring the prize increments to adjust the equation.

5.6 Difficulty Metrics

As rivalry for the prizes expands, the pace of arrangements found to the troublesome processing issue will increment. With more diggers scanning for the method, the average rate could turn out to be not exactly the expected pace of one new block like clockwork.

- Mining Equipment
- Mining Conditions
- Mining Pools
- Mining Shares

Mining Equipment

In Bitcoin's initial days, standard CPUs were utilized to register the hashes.

Remembered for the first Bitcoin customer was an element that permitted you to use the CPU to mine. At the beginning of Bitcoin, it was simple for a single CPU to acquire a full honor of bitcoin. As the number of diggers expanded, CPUs immediately got outdated for mining.

As mining rivalry expanded, programming was adjusted to use realistic preparing units (GPUs). GPUs are enhanced to perform numerical activities commonly quicker than CPUs. They are utilized to quicken the calculation of complex designs applications, for example, gaming and to deliver. Considering their enhancements, they are appropriate for playing out the numerical tasks expected to figure a hash rapidly.

The mining administrators frequently kept up racks of GPUs. A few designs cards could be associated with one PC. This brought about the age of a lot of warmth. To keep up top execution of the hardware, cooling units were required to keep it fresh. Soon after the GPUs were received as the norm for mining, PC chip produces started creating microchips that played out the hashing calculations legitimately. This brought about an enormous increment in the quantity of hash performed every second, with a small amount of the power needed. Initially, Field-Programmable Gate Arrays, (FPGAs) were designed and utilized for building the mining rigs. These are exceptionally coordinated chips that permit a software engineer to encode the equipment level guidance to be executed straightforwardly on the disk. They furnished the diggers with quick hashing speeds and utilized significantly less power.

Application-Specific Integrated Chips (ASICs), immediately turned into the hot thing for mining. These chips could perform billions of hashes for every second while utilizing far less force.

Mining Conditions

Due to the requests put on the gear, it must be kept in an appropriate situation to continue conditions for top performance. Most outstanding are the cooling prerequisites. Cooling might be required to keep up a consistent temperature for the gear to work. Ensure that you consider a cooling framework for your spending plan and design. Electricity use from both the hardware and the cooling must be surveyed and organized. Spotless and stable power is significant not to harm the equipment. Electrical spikes and high loads can make interferences in your mining operation. Constant checking of the gear is substantial. Personal time could bring about a much lower degree of profitability than foreseen. Therefore, it is normal for certain mining activities to make full memories staff to screen the conditions and keep up the gear.

Mining Pools

It is tough for a solitary ASIC digger to locate the fundamental confirmation of-work to procure the prizes from another block. This is particularly evident if each digger on the system is working independently too. Consequently, the odds of acquiring the bitcoin are either win big or bust concerning a solitary block prize. To improve the odds of winning the bitcoin, a methodology for mining called 'pooling' exists. The mining administrators can consolidate their aggregate capacity to frame mining pools. As a gathering, their odds of finding the hard to produce verification of-work become much better. After winning the prize, the pool consents to share the benefits dependent on the work contributed by the individual miners. Mining pools give lower fueled diggers a favorable position since it tends to be hard for them to gain a full block alone. While working as a component of a group, their figuring power is granted dependent on the measure of registering power gave.

Mining Shares

In a pool, the work is estimated in shares. One offer is given for each verification of-work submitted. Because of a mining pool, the verification of-work is acknowledged dependent on the least demanding trouble level. At the most straightforward trouble level, a lot bigger scope of nonce is qualified as the answer for the registering issue. Verification of-work created against a single trouble level is how the original diggers can demonstrate to the pool that they have been working. Eventually, when an offer meets the system's trouble level, the entire pool wins the prize, as it is partitioned and conveyed to the individual excavator's dependent on the suggestions submitted.

5.7 Fees and Payout

The mining pools charge expenses, typically extending from 0.5 per cent to 3.0 per cent, contingent upon the payout strategy. Because of the payout techniques, the mining pool administrator might be in danger from a digger who cheats about the offer announced. For the most part, the more hazards the mining works expect, the higher the fees. A round is typically utilized in the figuring and speaks to the current block being mined. After a new block has been discovered, the series is shot, and another is started. The payout from the mining administrator depends on different strategies. A few techniques are upgraded for speedier payouts, while others give motivations for new offers. The different methods are intended to diminish or forestall cheating. The mining pools utilize various strategies, alongside completive charges, to urge diggers to join their pool.

Mining contracts are accessible for individuals who wish to redistribute the mining procedure to another organization. Organizations offering Cloud Mining administrations permit one to buy an agreement for a measure of time and hash rate. The administration also works to the mining pool process. The favorable circumstances of cloud mining are self-evident, as the purchaser does not need to possess the gear, look after it, and manage its uptime. All the hardware is situated in a far-off server farm and is kept up by the cloud mining company. However, the purchaser must be careful. The profits on benefit can be lot lower than ordinary speculation. Besides, there have been tricks announced and misfortunes from pernicious organizations. Ensure that you do your examination on help before paying for any administrations or contracts.

5.8 Hardware Efficiency

Starting with the equipment, one must consider the hashing rate of the hardware against the power utilized. A fundamental equation for assessing the mining effectiveness would think about these two factors

Hashes every second/power utilization = productivity

Equipment productivity figures help assess the equipment. Know that the hash rates distributed by the merchants could change from the original prices. Furthermore, it might take some effort for the hardware to show up. Ensure that you do some examination on the gatherings to perceive what hash rates different clients are getting. One must look at the trouble rate against the accessible equipment to extend a gauge of the potential returns. Utilizing some straightforward math, the compensations from mining at a predefined hash rate can be evaluated.

We start with the hash rate

hashes = number of hashes every second

As there are 86,400 seconds in a day, we can compute the number of hashes every day.

Hashes per second / power consumption = efficiency

5.9 Choosing a Currency

When hoping to gauge productivity, it is essential to consider the cryptographic money with the best odds of making a benefit. Trouble level and conversion scale are the two significant factors involved. With more than 500 altcoins in presence, an excavator has a considerable arrangement of choices to look over. To help with dissecting the information, one can depend on individual instruments to help with the figurines.

5.10 Trade/Exchange Rates

The current swapping scale for the money you are mining is an erratic factor in computing mining benefit. Numerous diggers have an idealistic perspective on Bitcoin if possible, yet in the transient, the unpredictability prompts vulnerability with mining speculations.

Given the dangers, we can at present make some widespread suspicions and use number crunchers to give us a scope of returns. The Coiners site offers some valuable instruments for computing future profit dependent on hash rates, trouble, power expenses, and block rewards.

Setting up a Mining Client

After doing the best possible investigation of expenses and rate of profitability, one may choose if it is the ideal opportunity to continue with setting up a mining activity.

5.11 Requirements

In general, you will have to have the best possible conditions to set up a principal mining activity. To begin with, we will quickly cover the fundamentals capital, equipment, offices, and availability.

- Capital
- Hardware
- Facilities

Capital

Most quantifiable profit estimation for Bitcoin mining shows gainfulness over some undefined time frame, surpassing one year. The presumption made for the projection incorporates a steady swapping scale and trouble level. In any case, these two factors frequently change, which can genuinely influence substantial profits. Essential to beginning a mining activity is an adequate cash-flow to convey the business forward. Before beginning the endeavor, ensure you have enough money to take care of the expenses for at any rate for 1 to 2 years, considering the different anticipated conditions.

Hardware

The acquisition of equipment is one of the more unpredictable parts of mining. Equipment sellers are continually structuring and improving their hardware. Regularly, new gear is pre-sold with a while of delay purchase time. Without superior equipment, one cannot start mining. Subsequently, be confident you approach a not too lousy arrangement of hardware before making sure about the remainder of your mining operation.

Another perspective to consider when buying gear is the future estimation of the hardware-dependent on its presentation and operational life. Bitcoin mining hardware is changing quickly and can be obsolete inside a year. After its helpful life is done, you may need to exchange the gear or reuse it to move up to new and more impressive equipment. This was the sad aftereffect of a massive flood in excavators purchasing the GPU cards. Enormous requests of GPUs were bought and used to mine, however at the point when the ASIC chips showed up, and the GPUs were immediately supplanted. Many diggers wound up with vast amounts of equipment unusable for mining Bitcoin. A significant part of the gear was utilized for mining other altcoins or sold.

Facilities

Early mining aficionados began their mining tasks from their homes, frequently in save rooms, carports, or storm cellars. These tasks immediately developed into racks and racks of hardware, with fans continually running as make-move cooling systems. The manageability of these activities running from an individual home or a family rapidly decreases. In this manner, it is imperative to tie down a changeless spot to set up your mining racks with legitimate ventilation and cooling. Easy access to equipment is significant. The capacity to analyze and supplant the hardware should be there.

Assist with guaranteeing most extreme uptime of your mining activity. Likewise, one ought to think about the future extension of their mining activity. Make sure to prepare with space if you intend to become your operation. Your mining offices should incorporate a steady and clean force gracefully. The mining hardware will pull a consistent wattage.

Along these lines, it is essential to guarantee appropriate electrical cables, associations, and outlets to give sufficient wattage.

With all the hardware running at max throttle, the sound volume and vibrations can be an issue. Make a point to consider deciding for sound sealing the office if the unnecessary commotion is an issue for the neighbors. Finally, ensure that your offices are appropriately shielded from burglary and other natural components, for example, flooding and additionally tremors. It might be conceivable to have the offices and its hardware guaranteed. Make sure to check with your agent. While mining equipment can work consistently without interference, a speedy reaction from its administrators is critical to overseeing uptime. Equipment and programming disappointments can occur whenever. Without a snappy response, personal time can indeed influence gainfulness.

Picking the Product (Software)

When you have your equipment bought and arrangement with a PC, you will have to arrange the mining software. The mining programming will oversee interfacing with a mining pool and connecting with the equipment. Some portion of the procedure is relegating work from the mining pool to your mining gear and announcing the offers back to the pool. The two most well-known bundles are combiner and BFGMiner. Cgminer underpins ASIC and FPGA Bitcoin mining and is accessible for Windows, OS/X, and Linux. It bolsters interfacing with various mining pools.

Interfacing with a Mining Pool

There are numerous choices accessible for joining a mining pool, contingent upon your inclinations.

It would be best if you settled on an informed decision on which mining pool to utilize, because of the payout technique, the expenses charged, and how frequently a block prize is found. Different highlights that are ideal to have incorporate insights, simple withdrawal of assets, and different sorts of combined mining.

5.12 The Payout Technique

The payout technique can change between the mining pools. Check the method, and the expenses included to ensure they coordinate your hazard and capacity to sit tight for payouts. Contingent upon your mining activity's accessibility, the sort of payout may influence your prizes. For instance, the diggers who do not run stable mining activity will be rebuffed utilizing a score-based payout. This implies if your excavator gets detached for quite a while, your score may drop to zero. Also, consider the terms for the payout. Some mining pools discharge income naturally, while others may force a limit.

5.13 The Pool Charges

A few pools may charge an expense. The sum, for the most part, relies upon their evaluation of hazard and the highlights they offer. For the most part, paying no charges is ideal, yet now and again paying an expense could mean better odds of acquiring a block prize. For instance, Debit charges 3 per cent expenses; however, it pays for each tackled block, even it gets invalid.

The Pool Speed

The quantity of remunerations earned by a pool is legitimately identified with the general pool speed. The quicker the hash rate for the pool, the more blocks found. In the long haul, the pace of remunerations found will average out, yet with littler pools, you could hold up days or weeks to get a payout.

Additional Features

In the wake of recognizing the payout strategy, the expenses, and the speed that best suits your requirements, you can assess the pool's other list of capabilities. A few pools offer pleasant diagrams and measurements, or email notices and cautions.

5.14 Avoiding Large Pools

The bigger the pool size, the more worry there is for it to move toward the hypothetical 51% assault size. The enormous pools can rapidly bring fear in the community. Generally, diggers have more motivating force not to join a considerable pool as it decreases the general estimation of the system. Since the excavators are attempting to acquire bitcoin, they have an enthusiasm to keep the system working appropriately.

There was a case, right off the bat in 2014, in which the mining pool GHash.io arrived at 42% of the system. As the pool size was moving toward 51 per cent, numerous excavators started voicing the issue and the need to lessen the pool size. Inside 24 hours, many diggers had left the pool, carrying the volume down to 38 per cent.

Chapter 6 Investigating Alternative Coins

Bitcoin's prosperity has prompted the experimentation and transformation of its fundamental conventions and instruments. Since its delivery, there have been more than 500 elective coins propelled. Each coin expects the freedom to get from and change Bitcoin to actualize its minor departure from the first structure. In this part, we will take a gander at four inventive substitute coins (Litecoin, Namecoin, Peercoin, and Primecoin) to perceive how they have utilized the blockchain innovation to actualize different ideas and frameworks in a decentralized manner.

We will perceive how the elective coins can be utilized to store and approve discretionary snippets of data, for example, area names, open records, and digital resources. By basically changing the boundaries of the blockchain, it tends to be utilized to organize different pieces of data in a manner that is openly straightforward, simple to review, and shielded from control. With these qualities, designers have the instruments essential to make new and inventive frameworks.

With such a significant number of elective coins in presence today, how might one decide the authenticity of a specific coin? How would we inspect and look at the specialized and financial value of each coin? How would we influence an elective coin's unusual usage?

To respond to these inquiries, we start by investigating in what manner or capacity numerous coins appeared, and more significantly, how we can perceive which coins are deserving of premium.

6.1 Open Source Cash:

In the preceding sections, we have secured open source and have perceived how the designers can rapidly seed thought and distribute it, with the goal that others can help contribute. The eminent impact is the fast advancement of top-notch programming. At the point when designers from various foundations and viewpoints can cooperate, troublesome programming difficulties are immediately settled.

Bitcoin was propelled as an open-source venture from the beginning. Right off the bat, the designers were engaged with the bug fixes and upgrades. Satoshi Nakamoto was essential in planting the seed for Bitcoin, yet without a network of designers sharing and looking into the code, the measure of trust earned by the framework would have been restricted. The open-source approach motivates others to test.

Under two years after Bitcoin's dispatch, the leading elective coin, an elective test blockchain, showed up. It was known as the Bitcoin Testnet. Propelled in October of 2010, its motivation was to make an autonomous system and blockchain for testing purposes. The designers could go without much of a stretch.

The Testnet coins were acquired which were not planned to merit anything, to test apps. Yet, not long after its dispatch, individuals were utilizing the Testnet coins as genuine cash. In this manner, Tessnet2 was propelled by producing another beginning block. Soon after, Testnet3 was powered with certain upgrades and improvements for testing. With the capacity to fork Bitcoin's unique source code, the designers could rapidly and effectively start their elective coins or altcoins.

6.2 The Ascent of the Altcoin

As the enthusiasm for Bitcoin expanded, the engineers began proposing elective uses for the blockchain innovation. Right off the bat in 2011, a few new altcoins were propelled to exhibit this potential. With every altcoin, the engineers envisioned options in contrast to the necessary instruments that make Bitcoin work. Primarily, the alt-coin designers looked for approaches to improve the "confirmation-of-work" agreement framework, on which the mining was based.

Conventions were based, and approaches to improve the dispersion of coins. The other altcoins tried different things with the conceivable outcomes of utilizing blockchain innovation to assemble decentralized applications. The applications included decentralized stockpiling, code execution, and identification. For our assessment of altcoins, we will present a few long-running altcoins: Namecoin, Litecoin, Peercoin, and Primecoin.

Namecoin:

Perceived as the primary genuine alt-coin dependent on a fork of the Bitcoin source code, Namecoin is an altcoin that executes augmentations in its blockchain to permit the account of open name data for different applications. The first of these applications subbed for the Internet's space name framework (DNS).

Decentralized Area Name Administration:

The DNS is like a vast telephone directory. At the point when you type google into your Web program, a solicitation is made to the DNS workers requesting to determine the name to an IP address. The IP delivers are utilized to course data between two PCs on the Internet, like how the phone framework associates two telephone numbers together.

With the first DNS framework, the concentrated specialists had set up issue names, for example, Google or Wikipedia, to associations. Once bought, the association could adjust the rundown of workers that their area names made plans to.

There are some disputable issues depending on focal experts for DNS. Now and again, governments or large organizations can utilize their capacity to assume control over the DNS framework. Using their ability, they can block, edit, spy, or assume control over the DNS passages. Free discourse advocates guarantee this maltreatment of intensity is deceptive, and against the Internet client's entitlement to security and the option to get open data.

Namecoin offers a decentralized answer for this issue utilizing blockchain innovation. By purchasing namecoins, the clients can buy a. piece space name by experiencing a brought together assistance. With control of their area name through their private keys, the client can adjust or offer the rights to the space name without mediation.

Since the Namecoin blockchain is decentralized, no substance can bargain the framework or block the entrance. Many hubs, each containing a duplicate of the Namecoin blockchain, exist to serve and react to the DNS demands. Without unified support of bargain, it turns out to be extremely hard to control DNS.

As a certifiable model, Namecoins have demonstrated how a decentralized framework can supplant the unified associations on the Internet. In a period of many institutional interruptions, decentralized applications and administrations may fill in as a suitable substitution to help protect the privileges of Internet clients around the globe.

Namecoin is likewise perceived like the primary altcoin to present combined mining. To clarify blended mining, one can review a PC digging for bitcoins. Another block of exchanges is amassed, and a cryptographic capacity is applied to it until an answer for a troublesome test is found. When discovered, the arrangement is offered to the system as evidence of work. The diggers who are the first to submit verification of-work know about new coins.

In most cases, a devoted excavator can just mine each blockchain in turn. We can have numerous option blockchains viewing for this accessible mining power. A situation dependent on dedicated diggers has a few impacts. To begin with, it makes rivalry for the diggers between blockchains. Moreover, when attempting to dispatch another blockchain, for example, Namecoin, it could demonstrate hard to pull in an available number of excavators to bootstrap the framework. The essential explanation is that individuals do not have a motivating force to mine, something that is not valuable. Merged mining permits the confirmation of-work from one blockchain to fill in as evidence of-work for another also. In a model among Bitcoin and Namecoin, a digger scanning for namecoins can amass another block of namecoin exchanges and implant a summary of the block into another block of Bitcoin transactions.

The excavator at that point keeps figuring the cryptographic capacity for the Bitcoin hinder until a legitimate hash is found for either the Bitcoin trouble or the Namecoin difficulty.

If the evidence of-work hash is found for the Namecoin blockchain, the Namecoin block and the Bitcoin block are submitted as verification of-work. The digger is then granted new namecoins.

On the off chance that the substantial hash is for the Bitcoin trouble, the Bitcoin block is submitted as confirmation-of-work, as typical. Just the mixture from the Namecoin block is kept in the Bitcoin block. The digger is then granted new bitcoins. Eventually, the mining procedure continues as before without any progressions expected to the convention to help combined mining in conclusion, on the off chance that both are discovered, at that point the digger has granted both bitcoins and namecoins — merged mining use a similar figuring capacity to make sure about both the blockchains. In our previous model, Namecoin must be customized to acknowledge the Bitcoin hinder as evidence of-work. In any case, the Bitcoin conventions do not require any changes. The result is two autonomous blockchains ensured by similar processing power.

Litecoin:

As the second-biggest digital currency to date, as far as market capitalization, Litecoin has worked as a clone of the first Bitcoin programming. Charlie Lee, an ex-Google worker who is currently overseer of designing at Coinbase, forked the first Bitcoin-QT code and delivered it as Litecoin in October of 2011 with some further changes.

Block Rate:

Bitcoin is intended to convey another block around at regular intervals. Some had raised the issue that the affirmation time was excessively long. Therefore, Litecoin was propelled with an expanded block rate roughly at regular intervals. This gives Litecoin the slightly preferred position of lessening the affirmation time, which improves the client's understanding.

Litecoin can bolster higher exchange volumes because of the expanded number of blocks. A quicker block rate additionally infers that it is harder to twofold spend litecoins.

As multiple times more Litecoin blocks are delivered for each Bitcoin obstruct, the new affirmations decline the odds of dual spend.

Be that as it may, Bitcoin's mining system is a lot bigger and balances Litecoin's bit of leeway of having a higher block rate. As a weakness, the Litecoin organization produces a bigger blockchain with more stranded blocks than the Bitcoin arrangement.

The complete number of bitcoins is fixed at 84 million, four times the quantity of bitcoins. However, like Bitcoin, the volume of litecoins given through mining rewards parts like clockwork.

Peercoin:

Presented in August 2012, Peercoin is an altcoin that is, for the most part, dependent on the first Bitcoin programming. Preceding its delivery, an open declaration was made with the goal that everybody had a reasonable notification to take an interest in its public contribution. Peercoin's inventive thoughts helped increment the vitality effectiveness of securing the system with the point of considering more noteworthy long-haul scalability. During its dispatch, new peer coins went through a proof-of-work mining process.

To bitcoins. While the dispersion of peercoins is upheld through verification of-work mining, the coins can likewise go through a "stamping" process dependent on an elective circulation strategy called evidence-of-stake.

Verification of-Stake:

Bitcoin's mining procedure requires a lot of figuring capacity to produce the evidence-of-work expected to make a substantial block of affirmed exchanges. Planned as a choice to evidence-of-work, the verification-of-stake printing process gives new coins based on the minter's responsibility for existing coins.

In the Peercoin convention, the responsibility is estimated by a "coinage". The coin age is determined by duplicating the claimed number of coins with the number of days the coins have been held. To start seeking a block, a minter more likely than not possessed the coins for in any event 30 days. In this manner, more significant and more seasoned arrangements of coins have a more prominent potential to procure. To balance this, when a lot of coins have been utilized to acquire a block, they are reset, and 30 days must go before they are qualified for printing.

At that point, the stamping procedure compensates the miners relatively to the number of coins they own, with an objective of 1 per cent a year. In contrast to Bitcoin's fixed amount of coins, peer coins have a yearly expansion pace of 1 per cent a year. Compared to Bitcoin's longest running blockchain, the official chain in Peercoin depends on the string with the most elevated complete devoured coinage. The final product is a mining framework that requires far less figuring power than evidence of-work mining. The mining procedure is additionally conveyed to the individuals who hold the coins as opposed to the individuals who own superior mining hardware. This further level the open door for entry. Proof-of-stake is additionally professed to be impervious to 51 percent of assaults. As the responsibility is required for the assault, the expense exponentially increments. Contrasted and confirmation of-work mining, vast pools of excavators can solidify to overwhelm the network. While the Peercoin arrange has a specialized constraint of 2 billion coins, it is just vital for inward consistency. It is improbable that the breaking point will be reached. Furthermore, the confirmation of-stake expansion rate will keep on delivering new coins later.

Primecoin

Presented in July 2013, Primecoin utilizes an extraordinary technique for mining coins. Confirmation of-work is introduced to the system as prime numbers. Professing to be the central digital money planned with logical processing as its work, the excavators vie for primecoins via scanning for substantial prime numbers. There is no predefined breaking point to the number of primecoins, only the natural circulation dependent on the arrangement of prime numbers. The shortage of primecoins is set by the appropriation of prime numbers.

Inside a given set. While each affirmed Bitcoin block contains a nonce and hash arrangement, each Primecoin block contains a prime number set as the evidence of-work.

Another noteworthy distinction among Primecoin and Bitcoin is the system that oversees the trouble level. As opposed to utilizing a reasonable block rate determined after every 2,016 blocks, Primecoin alters the trouble to scan for prime number sets after each block with an objective pace of one block a moment. Primecoin's speedy change span permits quicker affirmation times, roughly 8–10 times faster than Bitcoin.

Prime Numbers:

The essential favorable position of Primecoin is the helpfulness of its evidence-of-work to established researchers. Prime numbers, as most know, are numbers distinguishable by one and itself. Prime numbers have practical applications in the cutting-edge world, including cryptography. For instance, RSA encryption utilizes huge prime numbers to permit two gatherings to trade mystery messages using two keys, a type of open key encryption.

As an overall outline, an open key is determined by duplicating two huge prime numbers. The private key, which is held in mystery, is created from the first two prime numbers. The open key would then be able to be shared to encode a message that must be unscrambled by the private key.

Then again, prime numbers assist mathematicians with examining the appropriation of excellent number sets. They help addressing the questions for example, "What is the biggest hole between two prime numbers?"

Mining Prime Numbers:

The primecoin organizes three strategies to scan for prime numbers: Cunningham Chain of the primary kind, Cunningham Chain of the following type, and Bi Twin Chains. Top number chains are sets of prime numbers with certain numerical qualities.

Primecoin digging includes looking for substantial arrangements of an actual length. Scanning for prime number chains turns out to be exponentially troublesome as the chain's length increments. Submitted as evidence of-work, it is anything but difficult to check the set utilizing the diggers on the system. Since incredibly huge prime numbers can be.

There is a most excellent size convention to guarantee productive confirmation of the sets. Primecoin diggers despite everything make a block of legitimate exchanges to be hashed by SHA256 and incorporate a nonce. This creates a proof-of-work hash like Bitcoin. With the hash esteem, the objective is then to locate a substantial arrangement of prime numbers. The prerequisite for the set is that the birthplace of the chain is numerous of the evidence of-work authentication.

The trouble for mining, which is balanced at each block, depends on the length of the chain. Primecoin propelled with an underlying trouble level of 7. This implies a string with seven primes must be found. Since the contrast between a set with 7 and 8 primes can be commonly more troublesome, a fragmentary trouble level is presented based on leftover portion esteem. The partial trouble level depends on the Fermat rest of the prime number set. For instance, with the trouble of 7.5, roughly 50% of the chain of length seven will be substantial while the other half will not be.

6.3 Conventions Based on the Bitcoin Blockchain

Bitcoin's plan permits engineers to encode little snippets of data into every exchange. Utilizing a predefined convention, designers can manufacture a completely new altcoin on the head of the current Bitcoin blockchain.

A few instances of blockchain conventions exist, each with various attributes. Utilizing these conventions, the designers can characterize different kinds of units of records, make resources and tokens, and move those using standard Bitcoin addresses.

This opens the blockchain to numerous helpful applications inside the business world. As a certifiable model, the NASDAQ was the leading open organization to give private value utilizing the Colored Coins convention. With an elevated level of straightforwardness, the capacity to handily review and oppose debasement and control and effectively trade resources using blockchain innovation may carry colossal worth and respectability to the budgetary world.

Computerized Resources:

With the capacity to give a remarkable identifier to the advantage, we can issue and track the responsibility for a certifiable property as an excellent resource. Utilizing open or publicly released conventions, we can without much of a stretch record the responsibility for advanced support, with its history, on the blockchain.

For instance, the Colored Coins convention permits the "labelling" of a Bitcoin's exchange yield as an issuance of a discretionary unit. Any ensuing exchange referencing the issuance exchange would then be able to be used as the group gave. Digital resources have numerous helpful cases. Responsibility for things, organization stocks, or tokens utilized for casting a ballot can be given, moved, and reviewed.

6.4 The Eventual Fate of Finance

Innovation has changed the world in significant manners. From the steam motor to PCs, to the Internet, we have seen stunning advances by the way we can improve through innovation. Following the past increases of change, Bitcoin can carry a similar size of progress to back. Since its dispatch, only months after the budgetary emergencies of 2008, Bitcoin has tested how we take a gander at cash and fund. This way, our past ideas of depending on brought together organizations to issue, store, and move some money are presently sketchy.

Based on what we have seen from the usage of new advances since the modern insurgency, a significant number of our money related organizations face considerable disturbance. The Blockchain's disseminated record has shown its capacity to supplant a lot of significant functions they presently administer.

However, to our advantage, as Blockchain's reception expands, we can hope to see more straightforwardness and believability on a worldwide scale.

Conclusion

Since its initiation, Bitcoin has been relatively unpredictable. However, because of its ongoing storm, there is an estimate that it would reach 5 million dollars by 2030 and the chance of getting a cut of the Bitcoin pie is going to be disputable. Bitcoin users expect 94% of all bitcoins to be dispatched by 2024. As the value is moving toward the height of 21 million, many hope the advantages will get using the creation of new blocks. Yet, if more bitcoins enter the distribution, it leads to an increase in trade charges.

Concerning blockchain development itself, it has several features, from banking to the Internet of Things (IoT). BI Intelligence considers that exchanges should substance out their blockchain IoT arrangements. Blockchain is a promising field that will change sections of the IoT and strengthen ways that provide a more prominent understanding of resources, tasks, and chains. It will likewise change how records and linked clinical gadgets keep and forward information.

Blockchain would not be used everywhere, yet by and large, it will be a part of the system that uses the equipment in the IoT munitions stockpile. Blockchain can help with tending to specific issues, improve work processes, and diminish costs, which are definitive objectives of any IoT venture. There are several ways of mining cryptocurrency.

One thing that must be done right away is to generate cryptocurrency storage. Choose the kind of cryptocurrency that you want to mine and search the wallet for that currency. You will have no issues in searching for coins like Ethereum, Bitcoin or Litecoin; however, if you want to invest in the less-known currencies, you might need to look for a bit until you find a reliable wallet.

Getting a safe and reliable wallet is the most critical job when you are beginning with cryptocurrency mining. Think if you would be mining for a year and all of your profits would be stolen only because you did not pay sufficient attention while picking the wallet and picked a questionable one that got hacked into.

Manufactured by Amazon.ca
Bolton, ON